Growing Up Wild
BEARS

For Ian James Hosbein, wishing him health
and happiness as he grows up.

The author would like to thank Dr. Gary Alt,
Black Bear Research Biologist, for sharing
his enthusiasm and expertise.

Author's Note: Although this book has only focused on northern bears, there are also bears that live in tropical parts of the world: the sloth bear, the sun bear, the spectacled bear, and the giant panda. These bears do not sleep to escape the weather and have some unusual traits. For example, the giant panda eats mainly bamboo. Sloth bears are especially adapted to eating termites—they have floppy lips and missing upper front teeth that help them slurp in the insects. Something all of the tropical bears have in common is that there are not many of them—a result of having to share space with growing human populations.

Photo Credits: Alissa Crandall 3; Gary Alt 4; Wayne Lynch 5, 7, 8, 9, 14, 15, 22-23, 28; Tom and Pat Leeson 11, 18, 24, 29, 30; Ron Kirchner 12; Erwin and Peggy Bauer 16, 17, 20, 21; Fred Bruemmer 27

Growing Up Wild: Bears by Sandra Markle. Copyright © 2000 by Sandra Markle.
Published by Atheneum Books for Young Readers, an imprint of Simon & Schuster's Children's Publishing division.
Reprinted by permission of the author. All rights reserved.

Houghton Mifflin Edition

Printed in China

ISBN–13: 978-0-618-93250-4
ISBN–10: 0-618-93250-X

1 2 3 4 5 6 7 8 9   SDP   15 14 13 12 11 10   09 08

Growing Up Wild
BEARS

Sandra Markle

HOUGHTON MIFFLIN   BOSTON

This is a black bear just a day old! Look how small and helpless it is—not much bigger than a can of soda pop. The baby's eyes are sealed shut and will remain that way until it is about six weeks old. It has no teeth, and its hair is too short to keep it warm.

Baby Bear's first job is to get warm and find food. Luckily, Mom is close by, but it's January and she is asleep. Like all northern bears, Mama Bear escapes the cold winter by going into a special sleep called hibernation. This winter she will wake up many times each day to nurse and groom her cub, but she herself will not eat for as long as six months.

After it's born, Baby Bear squeals until Mom lifts her big head. She licks her baby, warming him and cleaning away the sticky birth fluid coating his body. That way there will be no smell to attract the wolves that hunt all winter. Then she sleeps again. But with such a big mother and such a tiny baby inside the little rock den, she must be careful not to crush her cub.

Baby Bear has long claws to help him cling to Mama's thick fur as he blindly climbs over her body. He snuggles into the safe hollow of Mama's curled-up body and finds the warmest spot—one of her nipples. Heated by Mama's breath, he sucks in warm milk. Baby bears make a humming sound, called a nursing chuckle, while they suck. This lets Mama know her baby is well and contented.

A polar bear cub starts life in a den too, but its home is in a snowdrift. See the claw marks on the walls behind the cub? Mama Bear dug this den. Male polar bears hunt all winter long. Usually only females build dens, and they do so only to have a warm hiding place to give birth to one, two, or, very rarely, as many as four cubs.

This polar bear is three months old. Its eyes are open, its fur is thick enough to keep it warm, and it is big enough for the next step in growing up—leaving the den. Mama has clawed open the roof of the den to make getting out easy. She is hungry and ready to go hunting, but the cub lingers, unsure about leaving the only world it has known so far. Mama will need to coax her baby out.

These baby grizzly bears have just left their den for the outside world. Now their job is to find enough food to eat so they can grow bigger. Mama's milk will help. Imagine drinking a glass full of whipping cream! Bear's milk is even thicker and creamier than that. This fat gives the bear cubs the energy they need to grow quickly. In just a few months while Mama slept, her milk let her tiny babies change into these furry bundles of energy.

Bear cubs continue to nurse during the two years they spend with their mother, but over time they nurse less often. Although they will only have baby teeth for the first year, the teeth are strong enough to bite and chew. Mama shows her cubs what to eat, and like human toddlers, they try out a lot of new foods.

Brown bear cubs eat fish, roots, ants, blueberries, acorns, caribou, wildflowers, huckleberries, wild cherries, squirrels, crickets, and just about anything else they can find or that Mama catches. This bear family is in the middle of its lunch.

Besides growing bigger, a bear cub's other job is to stay alive. This black bear cub is doing what adult bears do when they want to check for danger—standing up on its hind legs for a better view. Its ears are perked up too as it listens for trouble.

Like most bears, the cub can probably see about as well as you can. It can see better than you can at night because its eyes are better able to detect images even when there is not much light. The cub's big ears are just right to catch sound waves. But the cub's nose is its best alarm system. The cub smells its mother and the flowers it's been munching. There is also an unfamiliar smell. Could it be a wolf or another adult bear? These are both bear cub enemies.

The first rule the mother black bear taught her baby was to head for the tree-tops in times of danger. This little bear digs in its sharp claws and climbs. It looks like it has forgotten rule two, though: Don't look down.

Ears flat against her head, mouth open wide and roaring, Mom charges to protect her baby. Look at her big, sharp teeth! When an angry bear attacks, it usually bites its enemy on the head, the neck, and the back over and over until the enemy runs away.

Bears usually try to avoid fights, but not when a cub's safety is at stake. Even with their mother's help, though, as many as a third of all bear cubs die before they are a year old.

Life is hardest for polar bear cubs. Their world is icy cold, and the cubs have less fat than adult bears, so they lose heat faster. Polar bear cubs need to eat a lot because they use up lots of food energy just keeping their bodies warm.

These cubs are not playing "king of the mountain" while Mom rests. Her body is an island of heat. By staying on top of her, they are able to stay warm. Mother polar bears help their cubs in other ways too. Sometimes they let their cubs ride on their backs when they have to cross open water. If you've ever felt chilled after swimming, you know staying dry also helps the polar bear cubs stay warm.

This polar bear family is headed for the sea ice, a jumble of rough ice off the Arctic coast. Mom will catch seals and maybe a walrus to share with her growing cubs. The sea ice is a polar bear grocery store, but it is also a dangerous place for cubs because it is the home of their biggest natural enemy—adult male polar bears. In this world where food is hard to find and it takes effort to hunt, the cubs are just another catch of the day to the male polar bear.

Mom stays alert, ready to fight, even though male polar bears are much bigger than females. Luckily, this male just moves on.

Growing up isn't all work. Sometimes it's play. This five-month-old grizzly cub is rolling and stretching as it plays with its feet. Besides having fun, the young bear is exercising its growing muscles.

Look at the cub's feet. Its soles and claws keep it from slipping when it walks and runs.

Mother bears play with their babies too. This mama grizzly and her cub are jaw-wrestling—grabbing each other's jaw and trying to tug the other down. Mama plays gently, having fun and showing her youngster how to wrestle. It's a skill that could help the cub survive as it grows up. Cubs play rougher with each other, pouncing and tumbling, nipping ears and biting noses.

Northern bears, like grizzlies and black bears, that grow up where summers get warm must deal with a nasty little enemy—the mosquito. By midsummer in parts of Alaska, the air is filled with buzzing swarms of these insects. When a cub settles down to a meal, bloodsucking mosquitoes crawl into its ears, alight on the rims of its eyes, and bite its tender nose.

This black bear cub climbed a tree to escape the mosquitoes. High in the branches, a cool breeze keeps the bugs away. Content, the cub takes a nap.

This grizzly cub tried to rid itself of the pesky mosquitoes by shaking its head and whining. Finally, the cub could stand it no longer and dashed into the stream, to run away from the buzzing, biting bugs. What the cub forgot was that it was also running away from Mama Bear.

Mom huffed and grunted, a sound that stopped the cub in its tracks and sent it running back to her side. During its first year, a cub is always close to its mother. Separation could be fatal, so Mom scolds the cub.

Now the growing polar bear cubs begin to hunt alongside Mom. They copy everything she does; they learn to find seagull nests, how to catch lemmings, and how to find seals.

As the summer warms up and the ice melts, polar bears may get too warm. To cool off, they lie down on their backs and wave their legs in the air. It looks funny, but it works. Polar bears are built to stay warm, with thick layers of fat and a thick fur coat. By lying on their backs, polar bears press the part of their bodies with the thickest fat layer against the cool ground. Fanning their legs speeds up heat loss.

All through the summer, polar bear cubs live mainly on their stored fat. They will do most of their eating once it's cold again and they can hunt on the ice. But summer and fall are one long feast for black bear and brown bear cubs. What they eat depends on their curiosity and what Mama Bear eats. It also depends on Mama Bear's home range, an area she travels over and over in search of food. More than one bear may share a home range that has a big food supply, such as alongside streams and rivers. Fish dinners help these grizzly cubs grow bigger and store fat they will need to get through the winter.

Before long, it will be time for the grizzly family to curl up together for their special winter sleep. So Mama teaches her cubs another lesson—how to choose a good den. It must stay dry and keep out cold winds. Before settling down for the winter, Mama Bear rakes grass and leaves into the den to build a bed.

While black bear and brown bear cubs are tucked safely away for the winter, polar bear cubs get their most important lesson—how to hunt for seals on the ice. The seals often dig caves into snowdrifts that form when the sea ice cracks and piles up into ridges. Mama leads the way, showing her cubs what to look for. Then she teaches her cubs how to sneak up on a seal. She also shows the cubs a good trick by waiting patiently next to a seal hole. Seals swim under the ice, but they are holding their breath. They must surface through a hole in the ice to breathe, so a bear that waits next to a seal hole has a good chance of catching a meal.

During its second year of life, the brown bear cubs continue their training, learning where to find food and how to get it. They are ready to catch their own food because they have their full set of adult teeth. Once cubs become young adults, they are on their own and are likely to share at least part of their mom's home range. That makes finding food easier when the cubs first have to start doing all the hunting for themselves.

Different bears have different hunting styles. For example, this mom catches salmon by standing in the water, head down, right at a spot where fish are likely to jump. When a fish does jump, the bear opens her mouth and catches the fish in her jaws. Other bears have other tricks, such as herding salmon into shallow water, where they are easier to catch, or diving down to pluck a tired salmon off the bottom. As adults, the young bears are likely to hunt just like Mom.

When a bear cub leaves its mother and sets off on its own depends on the youngster. Even two-year-olds will still nurse once in a while, but they do it less and less often. Some polar bear and brown bear cubs will stay with their mother for two and a half to three years. Most black bear cubs only stay with their mom for about a year and a half.

By the time her cubs have gone off on their own, Mother Bear will have mated again. Her babies will not start to grow, though, until she settles into her den for the winter. Just two months later, they will be born while she is in her special winter sleep. Then the growing-up process will begin all over again.

Glossary

ARCTIC (ärk ' tik, är '-) The region of ocean and land surrounding the North Pole. 15

BLACK BEAR (blak bâr) There are both Asiatic black bears and American black bears. A very adaptable bear, it commonly lives in forests close to people. Even though they are still called black bears, some of these bears are brown and some are even white. Native Americans believed these white bears had special powers. 4, 10–12, 19, 26

BROWN BEAR (broun bâr) This bear is found over a large range, including much of northwestern North America and northern parts of the former USSR and Eurasia. They also range from coastal areas to Arctic tundra. 9, 28-29, 30

CLAW (klô) The name given to animal toenails. Unlike a cat's claws, bear claws cannot be pulled back into a skin sheath. The front claws are usually longer than the back claws. 5, 12, 16

DEN (den) A shelter where a bear escapes from the cold, usually to spend the whole winter. A den may be in a hollow tree, a small cave, a snowdrift, or nearly any other place a bear can stay dry and shielded from cold winds. 4-8, 25, 30

ENEMY (en' e mē) A bear's enemy is any person or animal who would try to hurt or kill it. A full grown bear's enemies are mainly other bears and human hunters. The smaller the cub, the more enemies it has. 10, 13, 15, 21

GRIZZLY BEAR (griz ' lē bâr) A type of brown bear whose long guard hairs are tipped with white or tan—a sort of frosted look. 8, 16-18, 20-21, 25

MOSQUITO (mə sket ' o, -ə) A type of insect where the female has mouth parts designed to let it pierce animal skin to suck blood. Then it lays its eggs in water. The baby mosquitoes live near the surface of the water until they become adults and fly away. 19-21

MILK (milk) Food produced in the body of female mammals, animals that have hair and give birth to live young. Milk supplies food energy for the babies so they can grow big enough to eat other food. 5, 8

NIPPLE (nip ' l) The body part on a female that her baby sucks to get her milk. 5

NURSE (nʉrs) To feed on a mother's milk. 5, 8, 30

POLAR BEAR (po ' ler bâr) Largest of all the bears, males may be nearly as tall on all fours as some people. They range in color from silvery white to light yellow. They are found in northern marine areas from Alaska to Norway and Greenland and parts of Russia. 6-7, 14-15, 22-23, 30

SALMON (sam ' ə n) A large fish of the North Atlantic and Pacific Oceans. Salmon return from the ocean to the rivers and streams where they hatched to mate and for females to lay their eggs. Then the adults usually die. 29

SEALS (sēlz) Marine mammals that live in cold areas and feed on meat. Seals have webbed flippers to help them swim and smooth fur coats to keep them warm in the cold water. 15, 22-23, 26

WOLF (woolf) A large doglike animal that hunts in packs. Wolves attack and kill bear cubs if their mother does not protect them. 5, 10

WRESTLE (res ' 'l) To push and pull in a struggle. Bear cubs do this for fun. Adult bears jaw-wrestle over a mate or hunting territory. 17

ä as in cart	ā as in ape	â as in air	ə as in banana	ē as in even
i as in bite	ō as in go	ü as in rule	ʉ as in fur